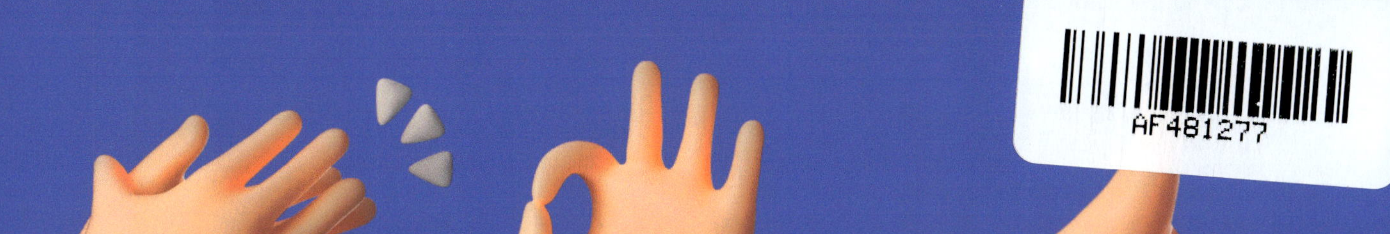
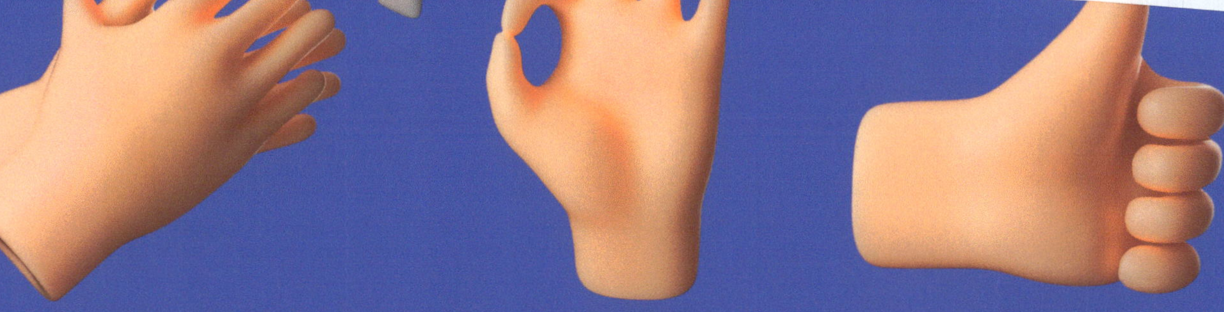

WHAT CAN MY HANDS SAY?

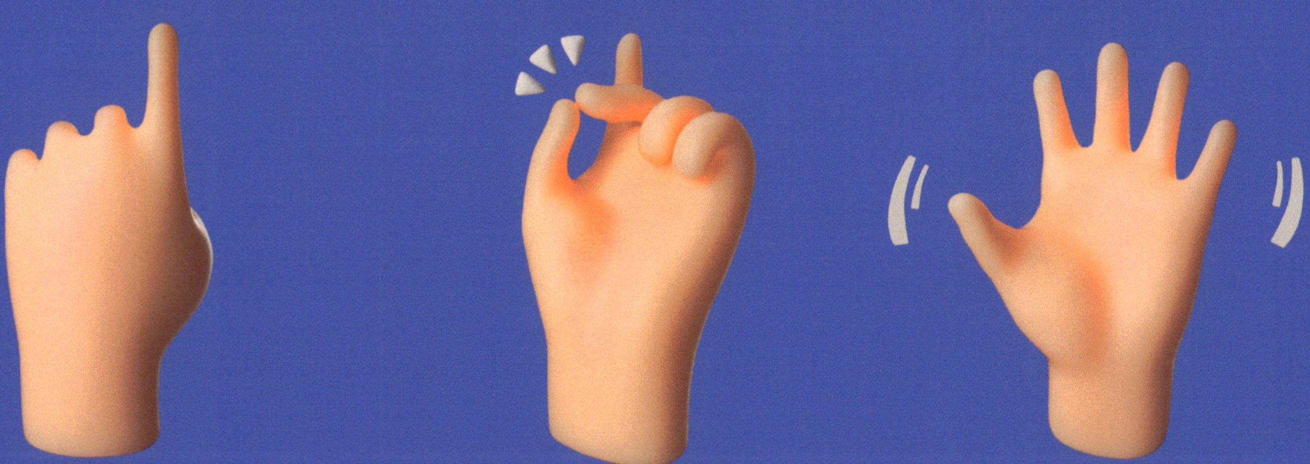

LOVE FROM ELLA

HELLO

GREET

I'M OVER HERE!

I LOVE YOU
ROCK AND ROLL
ROCK ON!

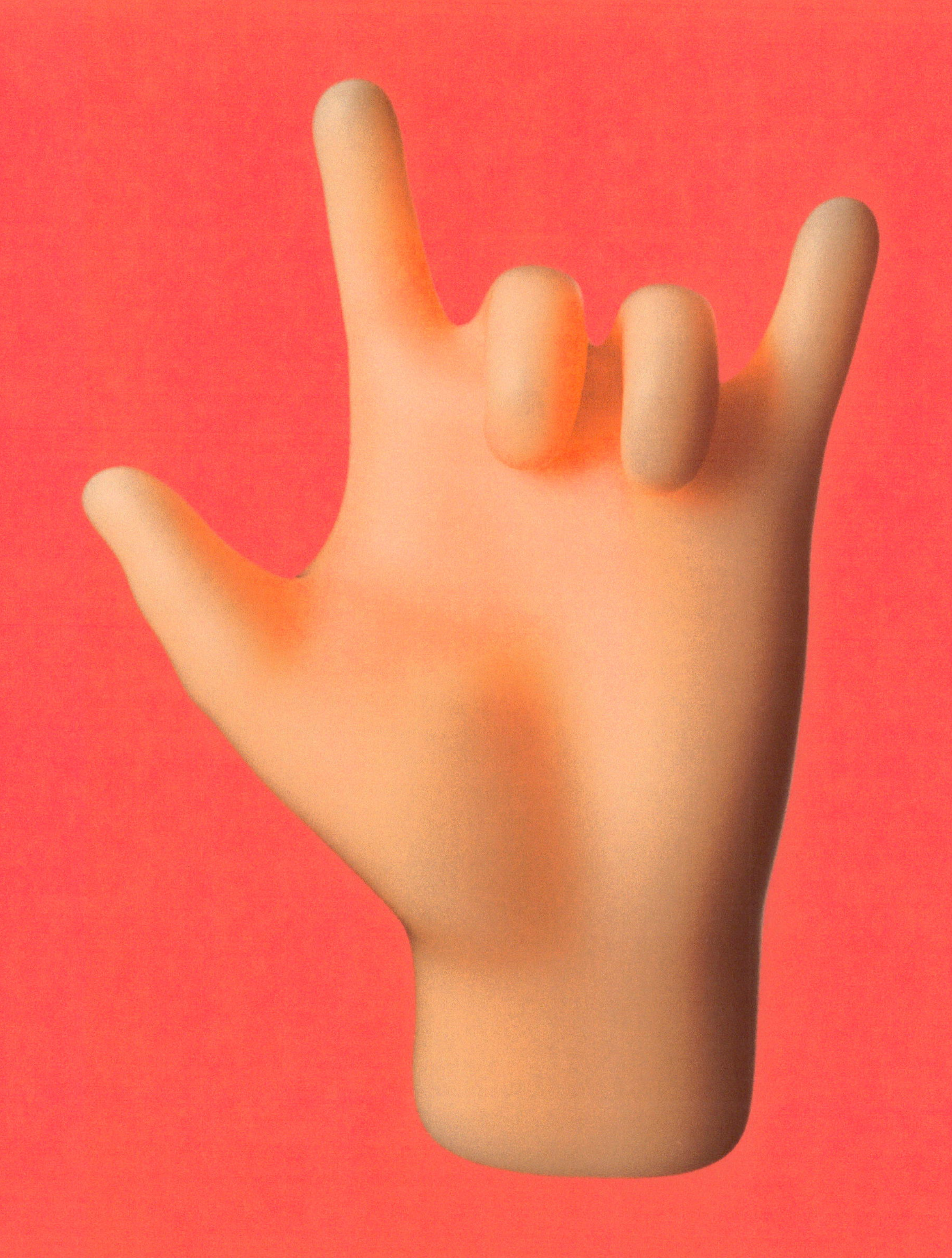

WELL DONE
I LIKE THAT!
CLAP TO THE BEAT

POINT

SHOW

DIRECT

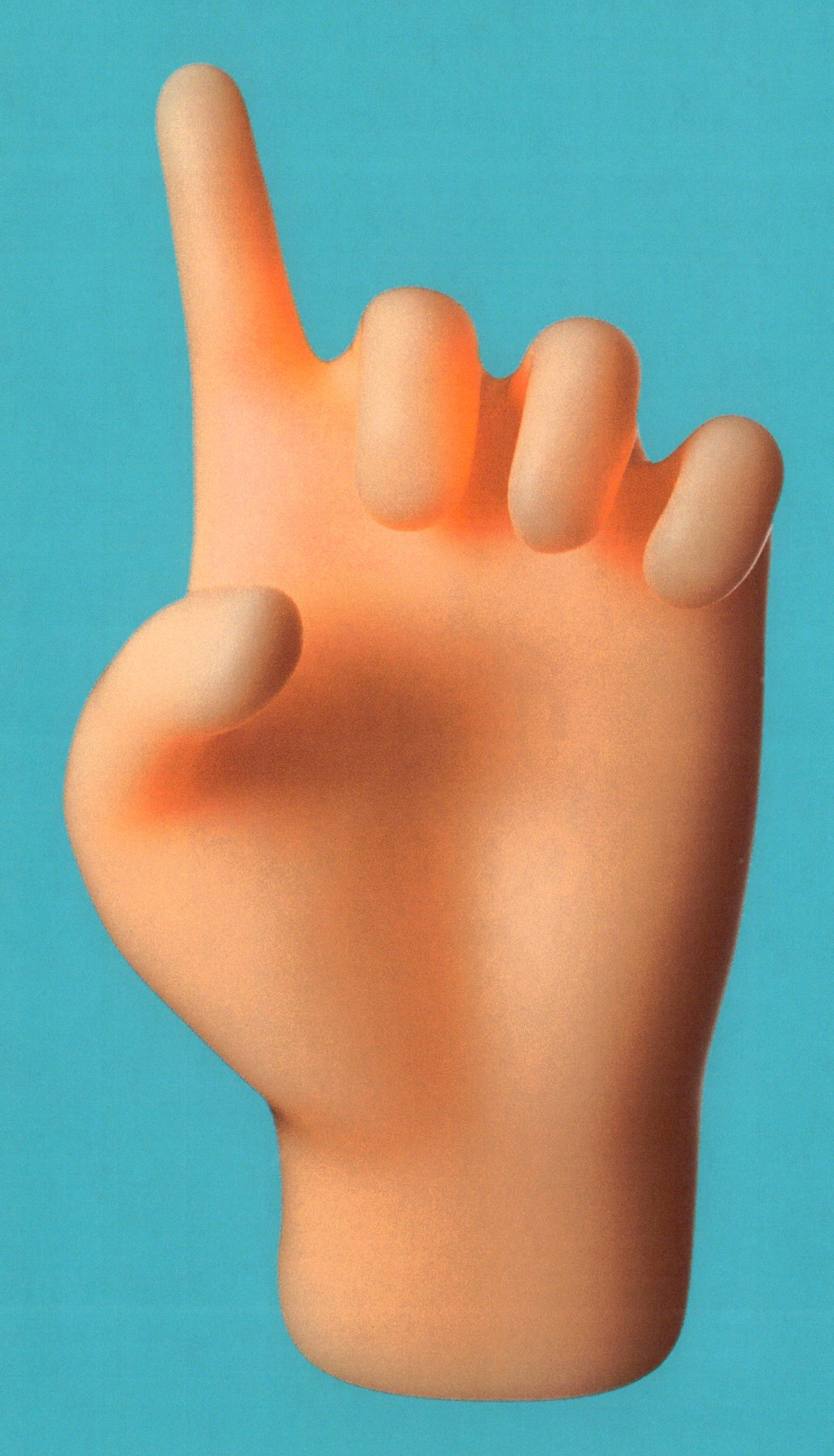

YES
I APPROVE
ENCOURAGE

OK
I'M A-OKAY
PERFECT

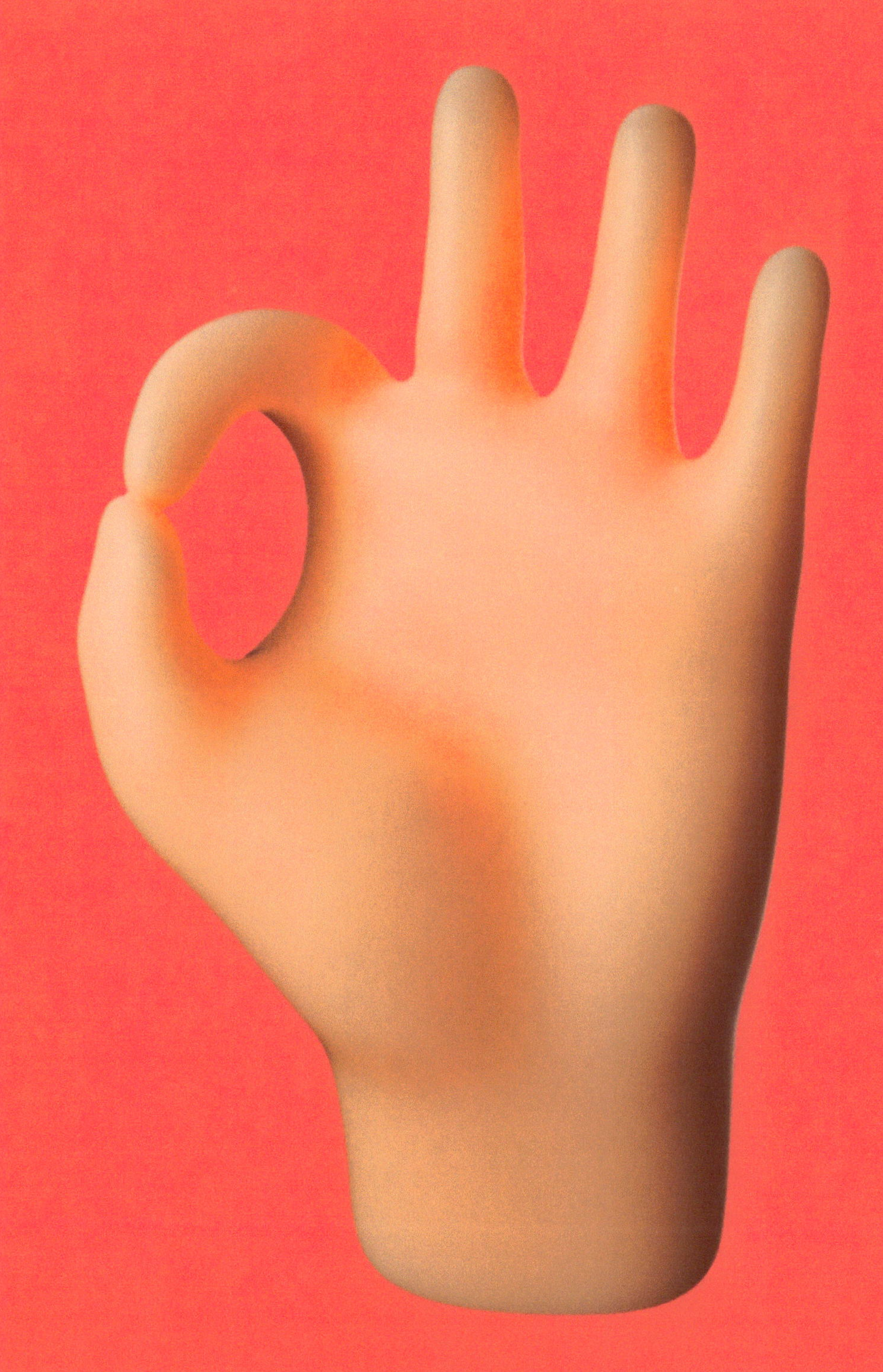

MAKE MUSIC
CLICK ON THE BEAT
CALL THE CAT

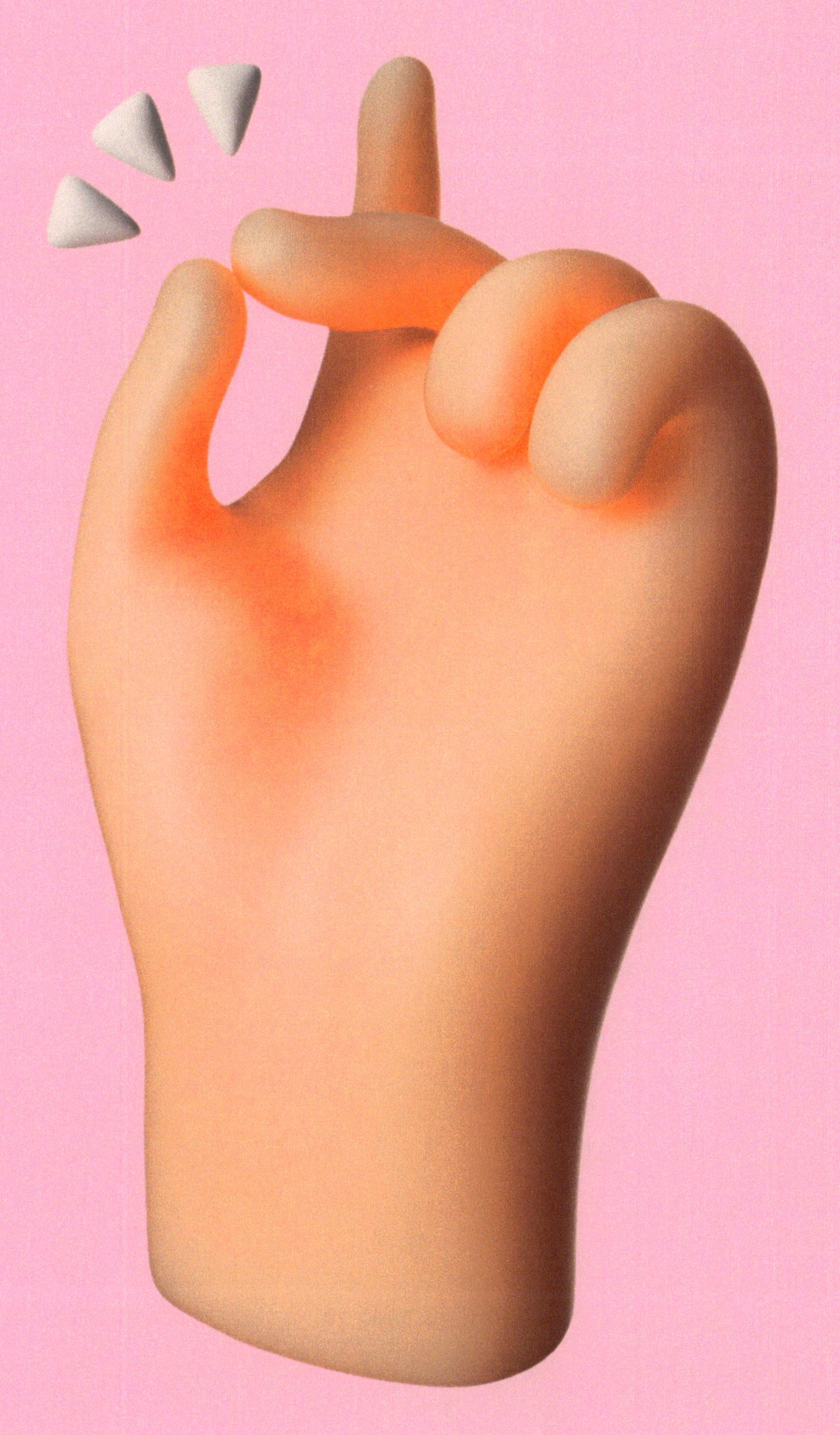

GREET FRIENDS
RESPECT
AGREE

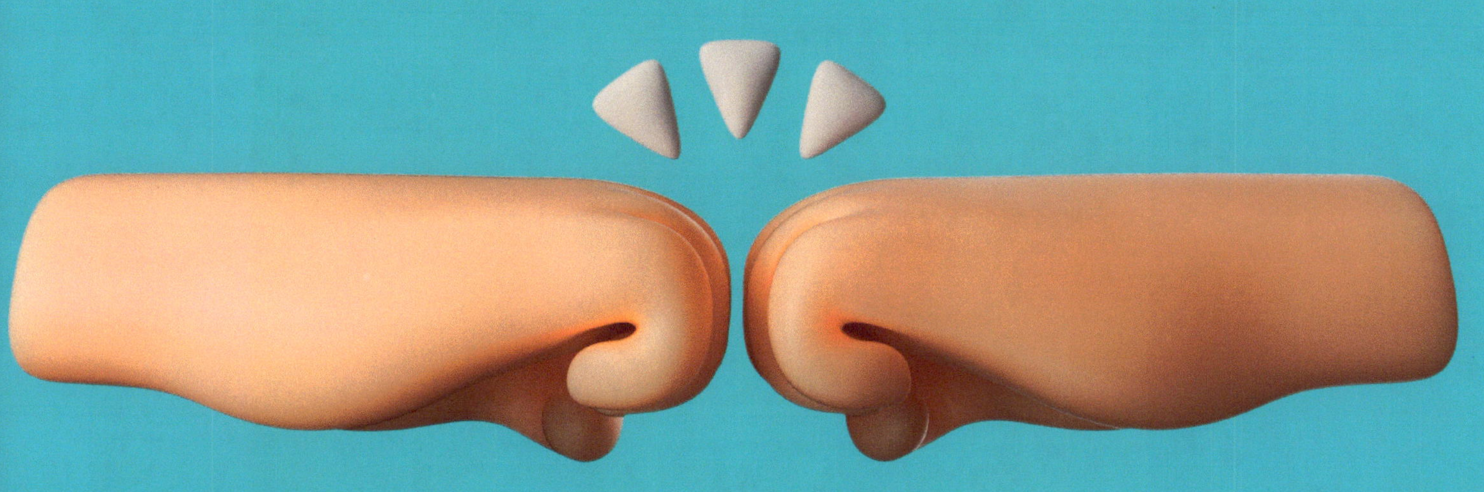

PEACE

FUN

CUTE

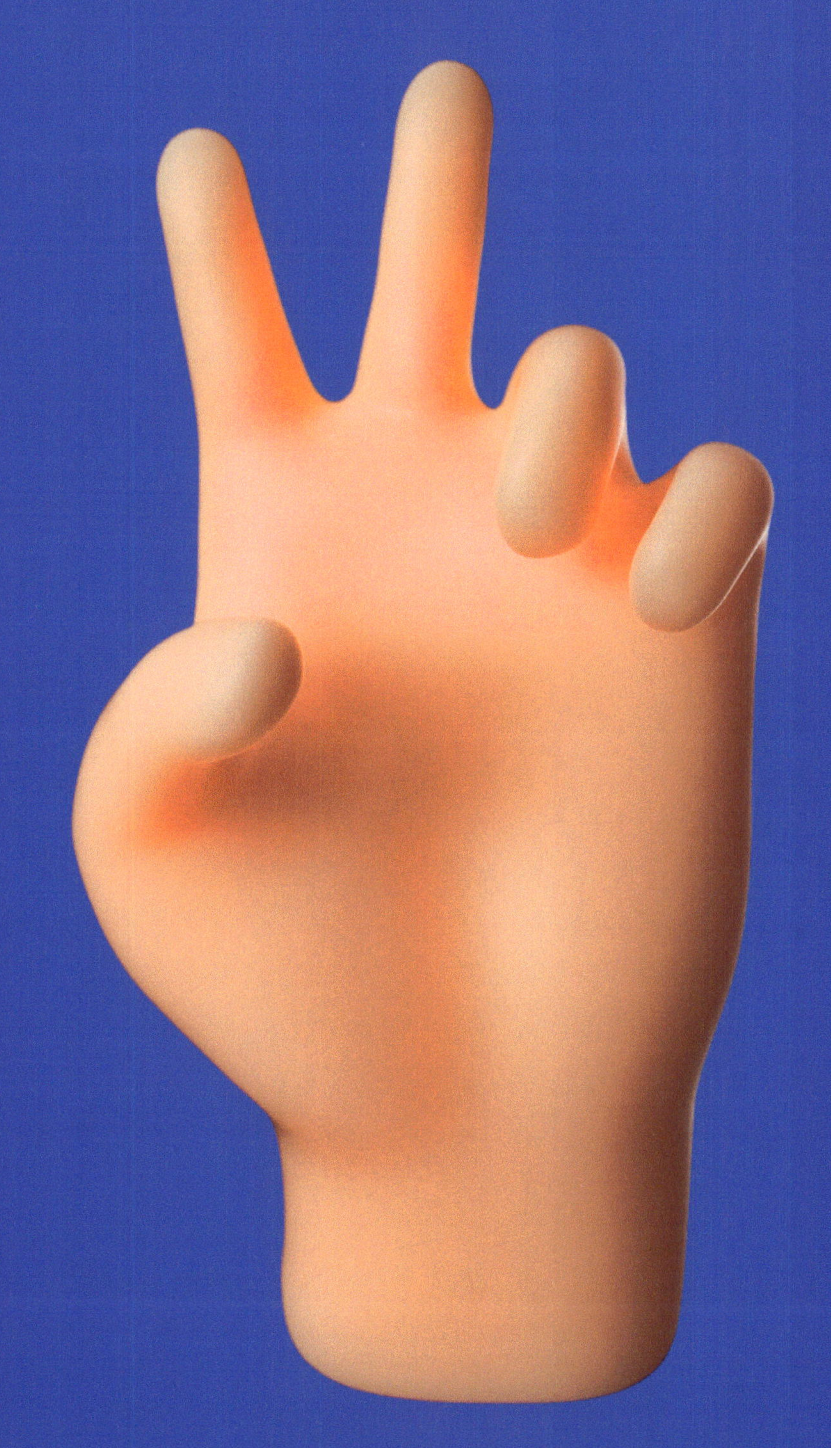

SENDING LOVE

HEART

HUG

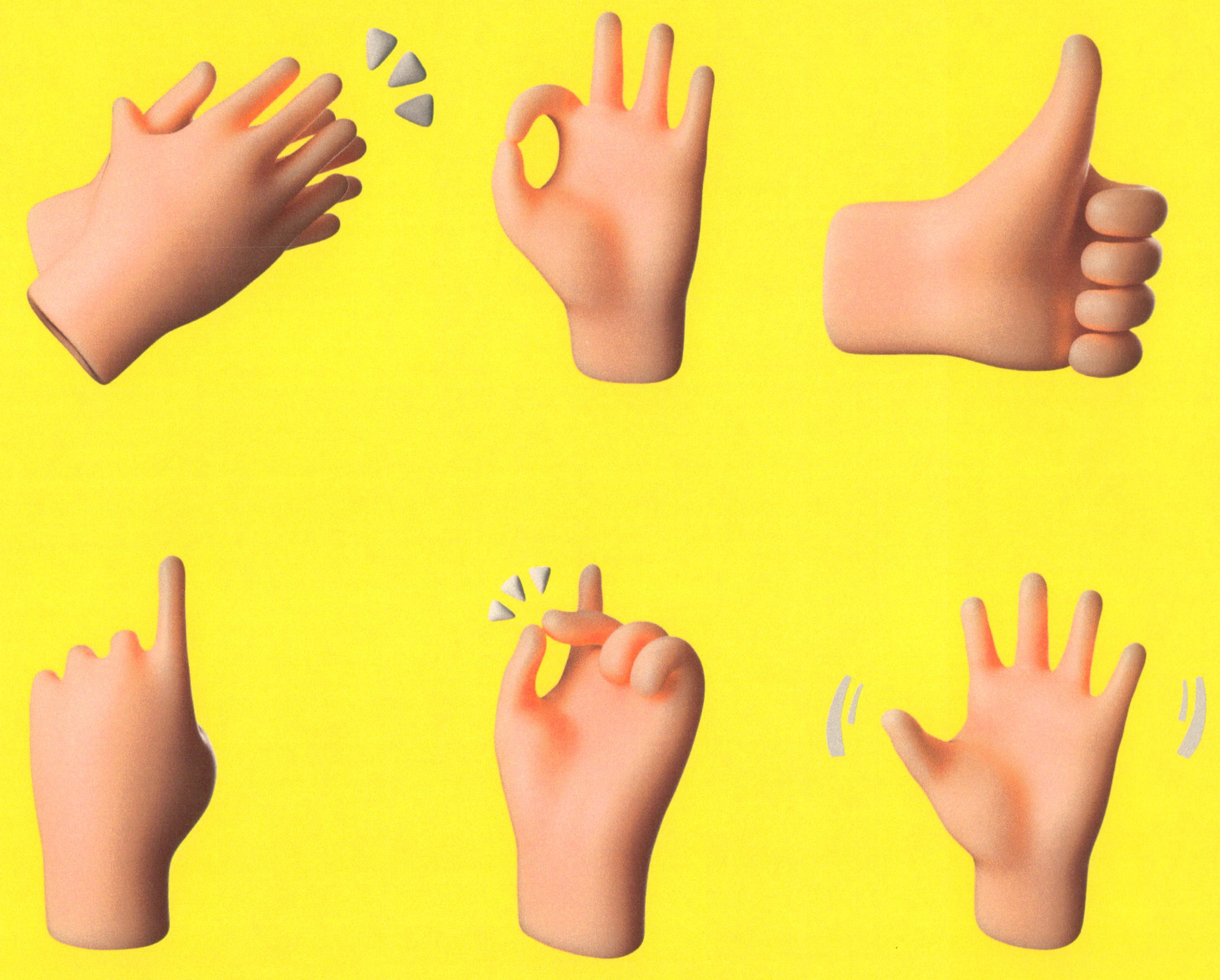

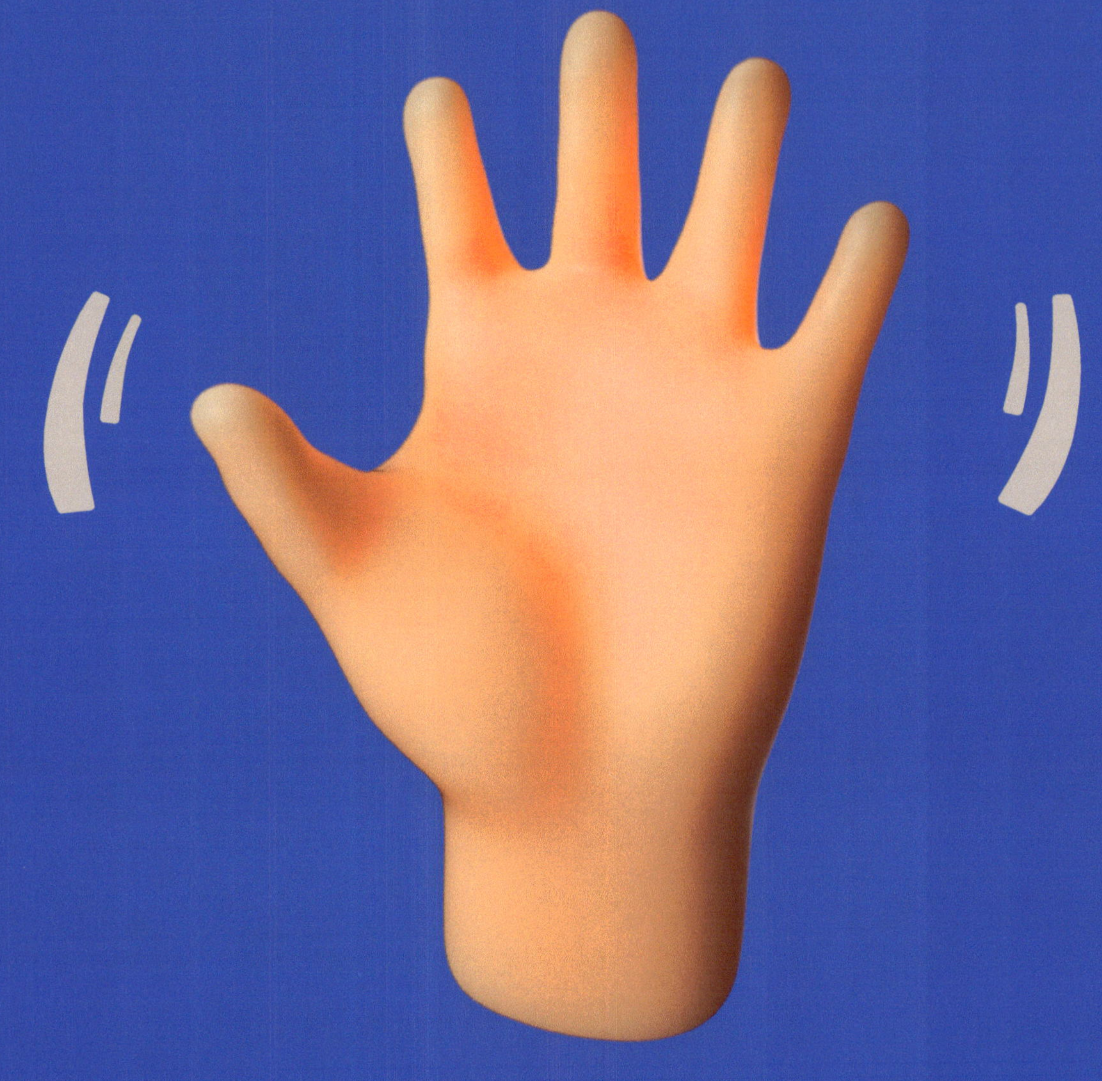

GOODBYE